LIONEL MESSI

This edition published in 2020 by:
The Rosen Publishing Group, Inc.
29 East 21st Street
New York, NY 10010

Cataloging-in-Publication Data

Names: Perez, Mike.
Title: Lionel Messi / Mike Perez.
Description: New York : Rosen YA, 2020. |
Series: Soccer superstars
Identifiers: ISBN 9781725340275 (pbk.) | ISBN
9781725340282 (library bound)
Subjects: LCSH: Messi, Lionel, 1987–
—Juvenile literature. | Soccer players—
Argentina—Biography—Juvenile literature.

Classification: LCC GV942.7.M398 P749 2019 |
DDC 796.334092 B—dc23

Manufactured in the United States of America

PICTURE CREDITS

The publishers would like to thank the following sources for their kind permission to reproduce the pictures in this book. The page numbers for each of the photographs are listed below, giving the page on which they appear in the book and any location indicator (T-top, B-bottom, C-center, L-left, R-right).

Cover photo: Alizada Studios/Shutterstock. Cover design element: pingebat/Shutterstock.
Getty Images: /AFP: 38T; /Alfieriphoto/LatinContent: 50; /Odd Andersen/AFP: 53; /Gonzalo Arroyo Moreno: 42; /Lars Baron/Bongarts: 19T, 30; /Sandra Behne/Bongarts: 44T; /Bagu Blanco: 5TR; /Shaun Botterill: 25B, 35T, 39; /Fabrice Coffrini/AFP: 58-59; /Phil Cole: 49T; /Mark Dadswell: 31T; /Denis Doyle: 17R, 28B, 59T; /Europa Press: 32R, 33R; /Frederick Florin/AFP: 46; /Stu Forster: 31BL; /Lluis Gene/AFP: 13, 14, 15, 17L, 22L, 23, 26T, 37T, 38B, 52B; /Laurence Griffiths: 4R, 36; /Matthias Hangst: 37B; /Scott Heavey: 22R; /Nicholas Kamm/AFP: 6; /Attila Kisbenedek/AFP: 44B; /Josep Lago/AFP: 20, 21B, 29TR, 32L, 41TL, 43, 58TL; /Bob Levey: 45B; /Alex Livesey: 27T; /Albert Llop/Anadolu Agency: 33BR; /Juan Mabromata/AFP: 44-45, 51TR; /Giuseppe Maffia/DPI/NurPhoto; /Angel Martinez: 27B; /Aris Messinis/ AFP: 18T, 18B, 19L; /Jeff Mitchell: 51TL; /Marwan Naamani/AFP: 16; /Koki Nagahama: 10L; /Leon Neal/ AFP: 34; /Jan Pitman: 33BL; /Manuel Queimadelos Alonso: 5BR; /David Ramos: 24, 26B, 28-29, 41R, 52T, 56, 60; /Miguel Riopa/AFP: 57B; /Ivan Romano/GC Images: 33T; /Gabriel Rossi/LatinContent: 47; /Miguel Ruiz: 25T; /Vladimir Rys Photography: 57T; /Piti A Sahakorn/LightRocket: 55; /Jewel Samad/ AFP: 31BR; /Dibyangshu Sarkar/AFP: 5BL; /Javier Soriano/AFP: 10-11, 21T, 35B; /Mehdi Taamallah/ AFP: 40; /Bob Thomas/Popperfoto: 51B; /Yoshikazu Tsuno/AFP: 54; /Urbanandsport/NurPhoto: 61; / VI Images: 7; /Jung Yeon-Je/AFP: 48, 49B. **Offside Sports Photography:** 12; /L'Equipe: 9T, 9B; / MarcaMedia: 4L, 8.

Every effort has been made to acknowledge correctly and contact the source and/or copyright holder of each picture and we apologize for any unintentional errors or omissions that will be corrected in future editions of this book.

LIONEL MESSI

Rosen
YA
New York

MIKE PEREZ

CONTENTS

INTRODUCTION

From the streets of Argentina to becoming the best player on the planet, the story of Lionel Messi is a soccer fairy tale.

Messi's story proves that it doesn't matter how big or strong you are, or how rich your parents are, or where you were born. Anything is possible if you are good enough and you work hard enough.

Messi has always had a special talent. That was obvious from an early age when he grabbed every chance he could to improve his skills, and soon the older boys were struggling to get the ball off him.

That has been the story all the way through Messi's life as helpless defenders struggle to stop him. When Messi is at his best, nobody can stop him. The number of goals he has scored and trophies he has won prove that.

By the end of the 2015/16 season the little magician had netted more league goals in Spain than anyone else. His incredible exploits brought him nine La Liga winner's medals, four Champions League triumphs, and three FIFA Club World Cup crowns by the end of 2018.

Even a medical problem that stopped him from growing properly as a child has not held Messi back. Barcelona were so eager to sign him that they paid for the injections that helped him grow and they have been rewarded in style.

It is why Messi will always be grateful to his club. Barcelona were the ones that helped turn his dream into reality as he made Spain his new home. The move to Europe could not have worked out much better. Soccer may never be lucky enough to see another player quite like Messi. He has been a true legend of the sport for more than a dozen years.

Children now want to be him, every player wants to be on the same team as him, and managers would all love to sign him.

Perfect role model

The success has not gone to his head either. Despite everything he has won, Messi remains modest about how good he is. It is not just his skill that is a shining example to everyone. His behavior and his attitude make Messi the perfect role model.

The striker has not forgotten his roots either. He had the chance to play for Spain, but Messi is proud to be from Argentina and said he could not imagine playing for any other country. He has many qualities to admire, and loyalty is one of them.

Soccer may never see another player quite like Messi. He is a true soccer superstar.

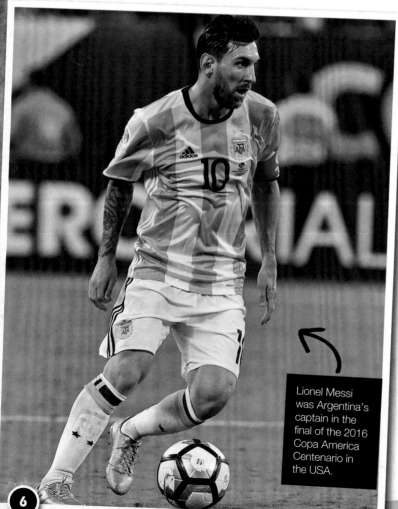

Lionel Messi was Argentina's captain in the final of the 2016 Copa America Centenario in the USA.

Lionel kisses the trophy after Barcelona won the Champions League crown in 2015.

EARLY YEARS

The little boy who became the world's greatest soccer player was born in a modest area and needed medicine to help him grow. When Barcelona paid for his treatment, his future was sealed.

Lionel Andrés Messi was born on June 24, 1987 in Rosario, Argentina. It was a time when Diego Maradona was the big superstar in the South American country. Around one year before Messi was born, Maradona had been captain of the national team that won the World Cup in Mexico.

He possessed many of the same skills as Messi has now and he was able to slalom past defenders like they weren't there. Many believed he was the greatest player there had ever been, along with Pelé of Brazil.

Just 12 months after Maradona inspired Argentina's success at Mexico '86, a new star was born.

Messi was the youngest of three brothers for parents Jorge, a steel factory worker, and Celia, a cleaner, while he also has a younger sister.

He lived in what he describes as "a nice, ordinary house" that his family still owns. Having received his first ball when he was around four years old, he started playing with his older brothers and cousins.

The house did not have a garden, so Messi would enjoy kicking the ball in the street outside his home in the run-down area in which they lived. It was not long before he joined neighborhood team Grandoli, where

his father Jorge was involved in the coaching and most of his family played at different levels. It was already clear Messi was a very special talent as other boys struggled to get the ball off him.

A shy and humble Messi kicked a ball at every opportunity outside the school classroom. At the age of eight, he went on to join the youth system of local professional club Newell's Old Boys. It was the club that Maradona had not long left as his own career was drawing to an end.

Expensive injections

However, just as obvious as his outstanding ability, it was becoming ever more apparent that Messi was smaller than most other boys. Around a year or so after joining Newell's Old Boys the doctors discovered he had a restrictive growth hormone deficiency, meaning he was not growing as much as he should.

The expensive injections to help him grow were paid for at first, but all that would change later. Messi's family were left with huge costs to pay for his continued treatment. Newell's Old Boys were unable to afford the bill and Argentina giants River Plate – a big club who were watching Messi – did not want to pay either.

In 2000, when he was 13 years old, Barcelona came into Messi's life to start a journey that would take him to the very top of the game. He was invited to Spain

"It wasn't difficult for me to move to Barcelona because I knew I had to. I needed money for my medicine to help me grow and Barcelona were the only club that offered."

Little Lionel feels the cold in a wading pool with his two older brothers.

for a 15-day trial and very quickly made an impression on Barça technical director Carles Rexach. He had nothing else to write on, so he agreed to sign Messi and pay for his medical bills in a contract that was written out on a paper napkin!

Messi and his father returned to Argentina where the rest of the family started packing their bags to leave South America for Barcelona, just as Maradona had done himself back in 1982.

"It wasn't difficult for me to move to Barcelona because I knew I had to," Messi said. "I needed money for my medicine to help me grow and Barcelona were the only club that offered. So as soon as they did, I knew I had to go."

The little four-year-old Messi (*standing, second from right*) was soon showing off his skills with local children's team Grandoli in his home city of Rosario. Below, he is second from right in the front row two years later.

MAKING OF A GENIUS

ATTITUDE

Often seen with a smile on his face and humble about his record-breaking achievements, Messi simply loves playing soccer. And he nearly always does so in the right way – with 100 percent commitment, honesty, and loyalty.

RESPONSIBILITY

Being the leading player on the planet is a heavy burden to carry, but it does not seem to affect Messi, who rarely produces anything less than his world-class best week in, week out.

LOW CENTER OF GRAVITY

He is a perfect example of how smaller players can use their size to their advantage. With superb balance and great lower-body strength, Messi is able to ride tackles, weave his way through the smallest of gaps, and change direction in a flash to leave opponents bamboozled.

THE WIZARD'S WAND

It often looks as if the ball is glued to Messi's left foot, such is the brilliance of dribbling and control. It is also a deadly weapon when it comes to shooting. Messi is equally capable of smashing home a screamer from long range as he is delicately chipping a helpless goalkeeper. A gold cast of Messi's left foot went on sale in Tokyo for more than $5.25 million (£3.4 million).

INTELLIGENCE

Messi's razor-sharp brain, combined with his natural talent and instinct, make him the ultimate attacking machine. He is ultra-cool when in goal scoring positions, rarely wasting any opportunity to find the back of the net, while he is also just as good at creating goals for teammates with his awesome passing.

DETERMINATION

Messi was told he would not make it as a professional soccer player as a youngster, but never gave up his dreams and has proved the doubters and critics wrong in spectacular fashion.

PACE

He is deceptively quick and his tremendous acceleration from the second he picks up the ball allows him to speed past defenders before they have a chance to react. Messi has admitted that being smaller has forced him to become faster, and there are few who can keep up with him when he is in full flight.

SPANISH ADVENTURE

Although small in stature, Messi did not take long to make a big impression at Barcelona after moving to Spain with his family.

Starting at the Spanish club's famous La Masia training academy – a sort of Hogwarts for talented young soccer players – Messi's raw natural ability was clear to see.

However, it was not all smooth sailing for the quiet and shy young South American in his first few years in Europe.

Messi had all the normal problems of trying to adapt to a new life in a new country. He suffered an ankle injury in his first season too, which ruled him out for a while. A delay in getting registered properly also delayed him being able to play competitive matches for Barcelona.

Swift and spectacular

He finally received his playing license from the Catalan Football Federation on March 6, 2001, and Barcelona wasted no time in giving him a chance to show what he could do, handing him his debut with the boys' team just 24 hours later. Those watching that day in the match against Amposta saw something that would become as regular as clockwork in the years that

followed – a Messi goal and a Barcelona win.

Messi's rise after that was swift and spectacular. As he grew in size and improved his stamina, Messi was increasingly able to show what he could do. He made his way up through the various youth ranks at Barcelona in lightning-quick fashion as he quickly proved himself good enough for the level above.

Josep Boada, one of Messi's first coaches at Barça, recalled: "He had an extra gear. If the top gear was fifth, he could find a sixth, and that meant at some times he was unstoppable."

Messi was initially played wide out left in the Barcelona youth teams, but he kept drifting into the middle. He was looking to become a playmaker who controlled matches and scored goals, like his idol Diego Maradona.

It was a playing style Barcelona fans have now become well accustomed to. After his rapid progress through Barcelona's youth teams on the back of an avalanche of goals, Messi soon found himself representing the club at Under-19 level despite still being much younger.

Messi (*front, second from left*) lines up with the Barcelona youth team. Also in the picture are Gerard Piqué (*back, fifth from left*) and Cesc Fàbregas (*back, third from right*) who would go on to become senior colleagues.

Messi pictured in one of his earliest La Liga appearances for Barcelona, against Albacete.

"He was small and skinny, but when he had the ball at his feet he had a tremendously competitive spirit."

Pere Gratacós, who was in charge of Barcelona's B side between 2003 and 2005, said of the young Messi: "He was an extraordinary player. He did things with ease, making difficult things look easy, and he did this regularly, it wasn't by chance. He was sensational.

"Physically he couldn't bring anything to the team. He was small and skinny, but when he had the ball at his feet he had a tremendously competitive spirit."

Then, still only 16 and yet to feature even for the club's reserve side, Messi was given his chance to play for Barcelona's first team.

Fine performance

Frank Rijkaard, Barça's head coach, was looking for squad players to boost numbers for a game against Porto in November 2003 and Messi – on Gratacós' recommendation – was one of those chosen by the Dutchman.

Messi only played the last 15 minutes of the match against the Portuguese side, but proved he was not out of his depth at that level with a fine performance.

Following his brief taste of first-team action, Messi then returned to Barcelona's reserve side to continue improving his skills, while at the same time joining up with the senior squad for training sessions on an increasingly regular basis.

Then, in October 2004, at the age of 17, Rijkaard deemed Messi ready to make his competitive debut for Barcelona in the derby against Espanyol – marking the start of what has become a legendary career.

THE BIG TIME

Messi may have been the young kid on the La Liga block, but he was head and shoulders above most of his opponents in terms of talent.

The question that still had to be answered was whether Messi could make the massive step up to first-team soccer. He would now be playing against men much older, much bigger, and much more experienced than him. Could he fulfill the remarkable promise he had been showing since he was a kid in Argentina? The answer to those questions has been a definite yes.

Such was his potential that Barcelona had no problems making Messi the second youngest player ever to appear for their first team when he took the field in the local derby against Espanyol.

Seven months later Messi earned himself another place in Barcelona history by becoming the club's youngest ever goal scorer. He achieved that against Albacete on May 1, 2005, when he picked up a scooped pass from Brazil star Ronaldinho before coolly lobbing the keeper. The Messi goal machine was up and running, and the record books were about to take a hammering.

As the months passed, Messi became stronger, more settled among the first-team superstars at Barça, and with it his influence started to grow. In his first season he played a small role as Barcelona became Spanish champions for the first time since 1999. He became more important the following year, 2006, as he helped the "Blaugrana" retain their league title and also reach the final of the Champions League.

Lengthy injury

That was the first time Barcelona had got to the European final since 1994, but although they lifted the trophy with a victory over Arsenal, Messi was left out of the match-day squad. That was a huge disappointment for the Argentine, who had been fit for the final after recovering from a lengthy injury. But, like in all good stories, there were always going to be setbacks and disappointments along the way. Injuries were a major frustration for Messi as his career developed, especially problems with his hamstrings. He was also criticized after punching the ball into the net during Barcelona's derby against Espanyol in 2007 – and getting away with it! That is not something Messi will look back on with pride, unlike two other games around the same time that showed the very best of him.

Still only a teenager, Messi proved there was something very special about him when he scored a stunning hat-trick for Barça

Celebrating becoming Barça's youngest ever goal scorer, against Albacete in 2005.

continued on page 16

Messi celebrates his first hat-trick by kissing the Barcelona shirt – and it was against deadly rivals Real Madrid.

The Club World Cup made it an incredible six competitions out of six for Barcelona in 2009.

continued from page 14

against their archrivals Real Madrid in a 3-3 draw. A month later, he then netted what could go down as the greatest goal of his career. It came against Getafe in a Copa del Rey (Spanish Cup) match and saw him run from inside his own half, beating half the opposition defense and also the keeper before putting the ball into the back of the net.

Messi continued to go from strength to strength in the following seasons, but while his star was on the rise, things were not going quite so well for Barcelona as a team. From being champions of Europe and Spain in 2006, they suddenly found themselves without a single trophy for the next two years.

It was a team on the decline, but that was all about to change when Pep Guardiola replaced Frank Rijkaard as head coach in the summer of 2008. Guardiola, the former Barcelona captain who had also come up through the youth ranks, decided changes were needed. One of the biggest changes was allowing Ronaldinho – voted as the best player in the world in 2004 and 2005 – to leave and give his coveted number 10 shirt to Messi, who had previously worn number 19. It was a huge honor and show of faith by Guardiola in the young Argentine, and Messi did not let him down.

With the likes of Andrés Iniesta and Xavi helping to get the very best out of Messi, Barcelona enjoyed the most successful period in their history as they won an astonishing 14 trophies in just four seasons under Guardiola. The highlight was in 2009 when they won all six tournaments they entered – the Primera Division, Champions League, Copa del Rey, Spanish Supercup, European Supercup, and Club World Cup.

Swamped with trophies

Messi played crucial roles in all those successes and as Barça found themselves swamped with trophies, he was finally recognized as the best player on the planet when he won the Ballon d'Or award for the first time in 2009. Most worrying for his rivals, Messi insisted in 2010 that there was still more to come from him.

"I don't think I've reached my peak yet. My aim is to keep improving day by day. I want to keep on growing (as a player)," he said.

And grow he did. In the years that followed, his rivalry with Cristiano Ronaldo for the accolade of being named the world's best player gripped the soccer world – with Messi picking up the Ballon d'Or on five occasions. It didn't take long before people were starting to talk about him as being the best player of all time.

Messi wore the number 19 shirt when he first made it into the Barcelona team, but he inherited the famous number 10 when Brazil star Ronaldinho left the club.

At right, in 2009, he was to succeed double winner Ronaldinho as world player of the year for the first time – and he got to show off his fashion sense!

YOUTH CLUB

With his career at Barcelona quickly gathering pace, Messi announced himself on the world stage in the 2005 FIFA World Youth Championship.

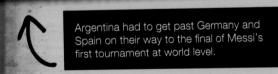

Argentina had to get past Germany and Spain on their way to the final of Messi's first tournament at world level.

Messi had made his Under-20 debut for Argentina in a game the year before, but was still to make his full debut for his country's senior team.

He was selected in his nation's squad to compete at the 2005 FIFA World Youth Championship, later called the Under-20 World Cup, that was taking place in Holland – and it was there that Messi made people outside Spain and Argentina really sit up and take notice.

However, the tournament could not have got off to a much worse start, as coach Francisco Ferraro's side lost 1-0 to the United States. Messi started on the bench – alongside teenage striker Sergio Agüero – and was sent on at the start of the second half, but it made no difference.

Argentina's second group game was against Egypt, and with Messi this time starting, he opened the scoring with his first goal of the competition just after half-time. Captain Pablo Zabaleta – later to star for Manchester City with Agüero – then added a second goal late on to secure a 2-0 victory.

Mazy runs

A 1-0 victory over Germany came next, although Messi failed to score and was subbed late in the game. That result meant Argentina finished second in their group and were through to the knockout stages.

Messi, already catching the eye with his fast, mazy runs and close ball control, produced his second goal of the tournament in a 2-1 win over Colombia in the second round. He won the ball himself, played a one-two as he burst into the area, escaped a challenge, and fired home.

In the quarter-finals, Argentina met a Spain team boasting the likes of Cesc Fàbregas and David Silva, but again they proved too strong and

Messi scores from the spot in the final against Nigeria and celebrates his first honor at international level.

triumphed 3-1. Messi netted the third goal of the tournament with a well-taken finish – just one day after his 18th birthday. Not a bad present!

And so it was Brazil, Argentina's great rivals, who lay in wait in the semi-finals. Messi showed no fear as he opened the scoring early on in a dramatic 2-1 win, picking up the ball 25 yards (23 m) out, taking a couple of touches inside and firing into the top corner for his fourth goal.

Golden Boot

Messi had inspired his nation to reach the final, where they would meet Nigeria, and he was not about to stop there. Shortly before half-time, he picked up the ball near the halfway line and set off on a trademark run that eventually saw him fouled in the area. He picked himself up and slotted home the resulting penalty.

Nigeria had no answer to Messi and he was upended again in the 75th minute before once more sending the goalkeeper the wrong way from the penalty spot to clinch a 2-1 victory – Argentina were the Under-20 World Cup champions for a fifth time.

It was Messi's first honor at the international level, while his six goals earned him the Golden Boot. His performances also secured the Golden Ball award that is handed to the star player, an accolade Argentina legend Diego Maradona himself won back in 1979.

EL CHAMPION 1

A glittering array of superstars have contributed to Barcelona's domination over recent years, including the likes of Ronaldinho, Samuel Eto'o, Xavi, and Andrés Iniesta, but the stand-out performer has undoubtedly been Messi.

Barcelona were without a Primera Division title in five years when Messi made his first-team debut in 2004, but in the subsequent seasons the Catalan giants have gone on to become the most revered club team in world soccer, collecting the Spanish league title on a staggering nine occasions through the 2017/18 season.

The first of those came in the 2004/05 season, although the young Messi only had a small hand in that success, with one goal from eight appearances, most of them as a substitute.

He made a much bigger contribution the following year, as Barcelona retained their title in emphatic fashion, finishing 12 points clear of their nearest rivals Real Madrid. That season Messi struck six times in 17 league games, and would almost certainly have got many more goals but for an injury that sidelined him for the final few months of the season.

Barcelona were then beaten to the title by Real Madrid for the next two seasons, despite Messi becoming an increasingly dominant force in the game with a series of superb performances.

After going two years without winning any competition, Barcelona decided to replace head coach Frank Rijkaard with Pep Guardiola in the summer of 2008. That marked the start of the greatest period in the club's history – with Messi central to their record-breaking success.

In the next three years, Barcelona would claim trophy after trophy, including three successive Primera Division titles.

In the 2008/09 season, they finished nine points clear of second-placed Real Madrid in a campaign that saw them score an incredible 105 goals. Messi grabbed 23 of them in 31 appearances.

Hottest property

The following season Messi scored 34 goals in 35 matches as Barça retained their title with a 99-point haul, losing just once in 38 games all season. Messi finished as the leading scorer in both the Primera Division and in Europe for the first time in his career, as well as equalling the club-record 34 goals Ronaldo scored for Barcelona in 1996/97.

Messi was now firmly established as the hottest property in the game and he was back among the goals in 2010/11 as Barcelona claimed a hat-trick of league titles.

Messi gets a champagne shower from teammate Gerard Piqué as they celebrate the 2008/09 title.

Messi addresses the fans as Barcelona celebrates the 2009/10 championship, before showing off the trophy with club president Joan Laporta at a pre-season match in August.

The Argentine found the back of the net 31 times in 33 league games, although he was outscored by Real Madrid superstar Cristiano Ronaldo, who scored 40 goals that season.

All things must come to an end, however, and although Messi himself was in record-breaking goal scoring form during the 2011/12 season, Barcelona were unable to win a fourth successive league title. José Mourinho's Real Madrid took their crown after becoming the first team in the history of La Liga to reach 100 points in a single campaign.

For Messi, though, this was the start of the most phenomenal 12 months by any player in history. The Argentine was simply unstoppable, setting record after record as Barcelona – under new coach Tito Vilanova (following the departure of Guardiola in the summer of 2012) – romped to the La Liga title.

At the start of 2012, Messi was awarded FIFA's Ballon d'Or as world player of the year for the third time in a row.

A trademark lob over the goalkeeper was one of an incredible five goals scored against German team Bayer Leverkusen, making Messi the first player ever to strike that many in a Champions League game.

SIMPLY THE BEST

The year of 2012 may have been a disappointing one for Barcelona, losing their Champions League and Premiera Division titles, but for Messi it was a personal triumph.

Not content to settle for what had gone before, Messi somehow found an extra gear and started rewriting the record books almost on a monthly basis. It started, as was becoming usual, with Messi being named the world's best player in FIFA's Ballon d'Or awards, winning the crown for the third successive year.

Then, after marking his 200th league appearance for Barcelona with four goals in a 5-1 win over Valencia, Messi scored his first hat-trick for Argentina in an international friendly win over Switzerland.

In March of 2012, Messi was celebrating two more amazing feats. He became the first player to score five times in a Champions League game,

as Barcelona thrashed Bayer Leverkusen 7-1. Then another Primera Division hat-trick, against Granada, saw him become Barcelona's all-time leading goal scorer in official games – at the age of just 24.

His second strike in that game saw him move on to 233 competitive goals for the club, one more than the previous record set by César Rodríguez during the 1940s and '50s. Barça coach Guardiola said: "We are witnessing the best player in every sense. He does everything, and he does it every three days."

Messi was not finished there, though. Not by a long way. He scored all four goals in the 4-0 derby

"My record stood for 40 years and now the best player in the world has broken it, and I'm delighted for him."

– Former West Germany striker Gerd Müller.

Messi celebrates his second goal against Granada in March 2012, which made him Barcelona's all-time record scorer – at the age of just 24.

demolition of Espanyol in May to finish the 2011/12 Primera Division season with a staggering 50 goals.

That was the most in Spanish history and also the most by a player to win the European Golden Shoe as the top scorer in Europe.

The goals continued to fly in as the year progressed, including another Argentina hat-trick, this time against archrivals Brazil, as Messi raced his way towards another long-standing record.

An incredible player

That was broken on December 9 when two goals against Real Betis saw Messi beat former West Germany and Bayern Munich striker Gerd Müller's record of 85 goals in a calendar year that he achieved in 1972. Müller said: "My record stood for 40 years – 85 goals in 60 games – and now the best player in the

world has broken it, and I'm delighted for him. He is an incredible player, gigantic."

Messi ended 2012 with 91 goals in all competitions for club and country, including nine hat-tricks, and the end of the year did not stop Messi's one-man attack on the record books either. His amazing exploits in 2012 inevitably saw him named as the best player in the world for the fourth successive time at the start of 2013 after again winning the FIFA Ballon d'Or – something nobody else has ever done.

But Messi's record-breaking antics did not end there. He continued his red-hot form to claim another place in the history books by becoming the first player ever to score in consecutive Primera Division matches against every other team in the division after netting for the 19th successive league game in a 2-2 draw with Celta Vigo.

ver the next few years, Messi was playing better than ever. Slamming in goal after goal, he seemed to be on a personal crusade to break as many records as possible.

Helped in no small part by Messi's red-hot form in front of goal, Barcelona romped to their 22nd La Liga title in 2012/13, losing only twice en route to finishing a massive 15 points clear of archrivals Real Madrid. Messi led the way in the league in both the goal scoring charts (with 46 goals – 12 more than Cristiano Ronaldo) and with assists (12). Barcelona reached the semi-finals in both the Champions League and the Copa del Rey, losing to Bayern Munich in the former and to Real Madrid in the latter.

Barcelona and Messi, under new coach Gerardo Martino, got their 2013/14 campaign off to a blistering start. On August 18, 2013, the opening game of the season, Messi chipped in with two goals and an assist in a 7-0 demolition of Levante. Two weeks later, Barcelona secured their first award of the season, beating Atlético Madrid on away goals to win the Supercopa de España. But the early promise soon faded. That was the only trophy Messi laid his hands on that season.

Treble joy

Having committed his long-term future to the club at the end of the previous season, Messi started the 2014/15 campaign as he had the previous one, by scoring two goals in Barcelona's opening game – this time a 3-0 victory over Elche. On September 27, 2014, he scored his 400th professional goal (still only 27 years old). Two weeks later, he netted twice in a 3-0 home victory over SD Eibar for his 250th goal in La Liga, taking him to within one goal of Telmo Zarra's all-time La Liga record haul of 251 goals. He surpassed Zarra's record when he scored a hat-trick in Barça's 5–1 rout of Sevilla on November 22. And the records did not end there. In February 2015, he broke Luís Figo's all-time La Liga record for the number of assists.

Whatever disappointment Messi must have felt after missing out on top honors in the 2014 FIFA Ballon d'Or, he did not show; instead, his magical form propelled Barcelona to a season to remember. On May 17, he scored the only goal of the game against Atlético Madrid to secure the league title. Two weeks later, he scored twice in Barcelona's 3-1 victory over Athletic Club at the Nou Camp to win the domestic double for the second time in his career. But the best was still to come.

In the Champions League final, against Juventus at the Olympiastadion in Berlin, Messi had a hand in all three of Barça's goals in a 3-1 victory. By winning,

Messi's teammates congratulate the Argentine maestro as he became La Liga's all-time leading goal scorer.

Messi and Barcelona romped to the La Liga title in 2014–15.

Messi played his hand in all three of Barcelona's goals as they won the 2015 Champions League final.

Barcelona had become the first team in history to win the treble of domestic league, domestic cup, and Champions League twice. And, on both occasions, Messi had been their star man.

It was the same story in 2015/16 as Messi continued to rip apart defenses in Spain and although Barcelona surrendered their Champions League title, they were unstoppable in La Liga and the Copa del Rey. It meant two more winner's medals for Messi's already impressive collection and yet another season of stylish success.

In 2017 and 2018, Messi won the Golden Boot for the fourth and fifth times as the top scorer across Europe's top leagues. Barcelona won the Copa del Rey both seasons as well. In 2017/18, Barcelona and Messi won yet another La Liga championship. Messi's importance to the team was highlighted as he was named captain for the 2018/19 season.

GREAT GOALS 1

Messi's career has been highlighted by loads of brilliant goals — some individual and some thanks to great teamwork. Here's a selection of the best.

BARCELONA 5, GETAFE 2
Spanish Copa del Rey, April 18, 2007

Messi has scored many memorable goals for club and country, but his amazing strike against Getafe in the Spanish Cup will take some beating.

Diego Maradona's famous second goal for Argentina in the 1986 World Cup quarter-final win over England is considered by many to be the best goal of all time, and Messi produced an almost identical effort for Barcelona 21 years later.

Picking up the ball 16 feet (5 m) inside his own half, the twinkle-toed magician skipped past two opposing defenders as he raced over the halfway line, and accelerated toward the edge of the Getafe box, where he evaded two more desperate attempts to stop him. There was still work to do, but Messi was not to be denied his wonder goal, cleverly rounding the goalkeeper before neatly dinking a right-footed shot over a sliding defender on the line.

BARCELONA 3, ARSENAL 1
Champions League, March 8, 2011

Many of Messi's best goals show just how good he is in all areas of the game. He can score many types of goals. Sometimes it is a mazy run, or a quick burst of pace or a powerful shot.

Messi gets much of the praise, but it is easy to forget that he is actually a member of one of the best teams ever at Barcelona. His teammates have also played big parts in many of Messi's goals, and one example of that was against Arsenal in a Champions League match at the Nou Camp.

The match was deep into injury time at the end of the first half when Andrés Iniesta made the most of a mistake by Cesc Fàbregas. Iniesta pinched the ball off the Arsenal midfielder and then produced a wonderful little pass to put Messi through inside the area. That was brilliant by Iniesta, but even better was to come from Messi. The Barcelona number 10 neatly controlled the ball before showing outrageous skill and confidence to loft the ball over Gunners keeper Manuel Almunia and volley into an empty net.

Messi volleys into an empty net to complete his brilliant Champions League goal against Arsenal.

Messi was still in his own half when he started to twist and turn past Getafe defenders.

REAL MADRID 0, BARCELONA 2
Champions League, April 27, 2011

Messi has enjoyed some memorable matches against Barça's archrivals Real Madrid over the years, and this was another one as he scored both goals in a famous Champions League victory at the Bernabéu.

His second, in the 87th minute, was a wonderful individual goal. He evaded the attentions of four Madrid defenders as he raced into the penalty area before sliding a low right-footed shot past Iker Casillas.

ATLÉTICO MADRID 1, BARCELONA 2
Primera Division, February 26, 2012

Messi is not only fantastic at dribbling and beating defenders, he is also pretty special from free-kicks.

One of his most memorable was against Atlético Madrid, when Messi showed both tremendous quick-thinking and fantastic skill to earn Barcelona an 81st-minute winner at the Vicente Calderón.

Standing over a free-kick on the left corner of the penalty area, Messi spotted Atlético goalkeeper Thibaut Courtois still lining up his wall. The Argentine took advantage to fire in a curling shot that found the top far right corner of the net with Courtois helpless.

Messi celebrates his remarkable free-kick against Atlético Madrid.

THAT'S A FACT 1

Nov. 16, 2003
Makes first-team debut in a friendly at Porto, aged 16.

Oct. 16, 2004
Appears in first official match for Barcelona in the 1-0 derby win over Espanyol. At the age of 17 years, three months, and 22 days, Messi becomes the second-youngest player to play a league game for Barcelona's first team.

May 1, 2005
Becomes youngest player to score for Barcelona in La Liga with his goal against Albacete.

March 10, 2007
Scores first senior hat-trick for club at age 19 and does it in style against Barcelona's archrivals Real Madrid at the Nou Camp. All of Messi's goals were equalizers with the final one coming in the last minute and earning Barcelona, who were down to 10 men, a 3-3 draw.

Dec. 1, 2009
Scores winning goal in extra time to earn Barcelona their first Club World Cup title with a 2-1 win over Estudiantes in Abu Dhabi. It also saw Barcelona earn another record by lifting their sixth trophy in 2009 – winning every competition they entered.

March 20, 2012
Becomes Barcelona's all-time leading goal scorer after scoring twice in the Primera Division match with Granada. Messi's second goal in the match saw him move on to 233 official goals, one more than the previous record set by César Rodríguez during the 1940s and '50s.

May 27, 2009
Messi's header against Manchester United helped Barcelona win the Champions League title and in the process secure their first-ever treble, having already won the league and cup titles that season.

Nov. 22, 2014
Scores hat-trick in Barcelona's 5–1 victory over Sevilla to become the La Liga's all-time leading goal scorer (with 253 goals).

June 6, 2015
Plays a part in all three goals as Barcelona beat Juventus 3–1 in the Champions League final - victory sees Barça become the only team in history to win the treble twice.

Feb. 17, 2016
The Argentinean reaches the 300 league goals milestone for the club when he finds the back of the net in a 3-1 win against Sporting Gijón.

April 17, 2016
Messi scores his 500th career goal for club and country against Valencia in La Liga.

Sept. 13, 2016
The star hits a UEFA Champions League hat-trick against Celtic at the Nou Camp. It's his record-breaking sixth treble in the competition.

OLYMPIC GOLD

Messi's greatest international achievement to date came in 2008 when he helped lead Argentina to the gold medal at the Beijing Olympic Games.

Messi's chance to be involved in Beijing was in doubt right up until his nation's opening game of the tournament. The day before, Barcelona won a court battle against FIFA, who insisted that clubs must release players under the age of 23 for the Games.

That meant Barcelona could stop Messi playing, but he was picked to start for Argentina against the Ivory Coast and swept home the opening goal just before half-time before setting up Lautaro Acosta's late winner in a 2-1 triumph. It was only after the match

that it was revealed Messi had asked to stay at the Olympics in a chat with Barcelona's new coach Pep Guardiola, who allowed the 21-year-old to stay in China and compete for his country.

Messi failed to find the net in the subsequent 1-0 win over Australia, and with Argentina safely through to the quarter-finals, he was left on the bench for a 2-0 victory over Serbia.

But, as at the Under-20 World Cup three years earlier, he had already shown the kind of skills that were capturing the imagination of the soccer world amid a talented Argentina team boasting the likes of Pablo Zabaleta, Juan Riquelme, Javier Mascherano, Sergio Agüero, and Ángel Di María.

Holland were the opposition in the quarter-finals and Messi was again on the score sheet, charging down a loose ball before bursting through on the edge of the penalty area and going around the keeper to score.

Great through-ball

The match went to extra time though, before Messi was involved in the winner as he set up Di María with a great through-ball to clinch a tough 2-1 victory.

As in 2005, Brazil and Nigeria stood in the way of success, but their great South American rivals – led by recently departed Barça teammate Ronaldinho – proved little test in the semi-finals as Argentina easily triumphed 3-0.

Messi, in the biggest game of his international career so far, did not disappoint in the Olympic final against Nigeria, capping a fine individual display with the pass for Di María's match-winning second-half chip.

Argentina had successfully defended their Olympic crown – and gold medalist Messi was the star of the show.

Messi consoles former Barcelona teammate Ronaldinho, who was captain of Brazil, after the semi-final.

It's a golden moment as Messi (*far left*) dances on the top step of the podium in the Olympic medal ceremony and then kisses his precious gold medal.

Messi soaks up the atmosphere at the medal ceremony in Beijing.

OFF DUTY

Messi is all-action on the field and rarely misses a match, but the superstar knows how to relax when he does get some time off from soccer.

Messi may be a genius soccer player, but he is also a doting father to his son Thiago.

Messi and girlfriend Antonella Roccu are all dressed up for teammate Ano Iniesta's wedding at a Spanish castle

With a statue of Adi Dassl founder of the sportswear company Adidas.

Lionel Messi attracts a gaggle of well-wishers, even though he's just out and about doing some shopping.

Soaking up the sun with Antonella on a yacht off Ibiza.

Seen with his 2016 Audi Q7, Messi has a collection of cars that include a Ferrari F430 Spider, a Maserati GranTurismo, and a Dodge Charger.

EUROSTAR

Barcelona had only won one European Cup title in their history – against Sampdoria at Wembley back in 1992 – before Messi's arrival at the Nou Camp, but that statistic was soon about to change.

The first of the four Champions League winner's medals Messi has won so far came in 2006. Despite still being a teenager, he was a regular in Barcelona's team for the early part of the tournament and scored against Greek team Panathinaikos in the group stages. However, he suffered a thigh injury during the quarter-final against Chelsea and was deemed unfit to play in the final, in which Barcelona beat another English team, Arsenal, 2-1 in Paris.

Messi was bitterly disappointed not to have been involved in that game, but he got another chance in 2009 after helping Barcelona reach the final again, and he was determined not to waste the opportunity.

Messi scored nine goals in the competition that season, but his most important by far was his header in the final that sealed a 2-0 victory over Manchester United in Rome.

Barcelona were knocked out at the semi-final stage the following year, losing to eventual winners Inter Milan, but the Nou Camp club did not have to wait much longer to get their hands on the trophy again as Messi earned his third winner's medal in 2011 – and

Manchester United were again the victims.

Messi netted in every round, including both goals as Barcelona beat rivals Real Madrid 2-0 away from home in the semi-finals, and he was again on the score sheet in the final as his side triumphed 3-1 over United at Wembley.

Back on top

Messi was unable to inspire another Champions League final appearance in 2012, 2013, or 2014 as Barcelona were dumped out first by Chelsea and then by Bayern Munich (in the semi-finals) and then by Atlético Madrid (in the quarter-finals).

But it was an altogether different story in 2015. On November 25, he scored a hat-trick against APOEL to become the competition's all-time leading goal scorer. Typically, Messi shone for Barcelona when it really mattered. Barcelona marched through the competition and faced Bayern Munich in the semi-finals. The Germans held firm for 77 minutes in the first leg at the Camp Nou, before Messi scored twice and provided an assist in a 3-0 victory that rendered the contest effectively over. He played a part in all three of Barcelona's goals in the final, too, as the Catalans eased to a 3-1 victory over Juventus in Berlin. It was the Argentine's fourth Champions League winner's medal – and it seems as though there will be plenty more of them to come.

Barcelona fans let Messi go to their heads as they arrive at Wembley Stadium for the 2011 Champions League final against Manchester United.

Manchester United goalkeeper Edwin van der Sar looks horrified as Messi gets up to head the second goal in the 2009 final.

Back home in Barcelona, Messi celebrates with his victorious Barça teammates.

"Lionel is the best player I've ever seen, probably the best ever. He made the difference. Messi is unique, a one-off."

– Pep Guardiola after the 2011 final

CHAMPION AGAIN

Messi was on target again when Barcelona and Manchester United came face to face once more in the 2011 Champions League final, this time at Wembley. He got one of the goals in Barça's 3-1 victory – and celebrated in typical fashion.

(*From left to right*): The Barcelona forward line of Suárez, Messi, and Neymar was too hot to handle for most of the Catalan's Champions League opponents in 2014–15.

EXPERT VIEW

Messi has enthralled and amazed soccer fans all over the world with his silky skills and awesome ability, but he has also made a huge impression on his fellow professionals. Here's what they say about him:

Tito Vilanova
Former Barcelona coach

"We do not know his limits. You should see how he trains every day – that urge he has to keep getting better. I think we will never see another player like this. He is the best in the world by far."

Samuel Eto'o
Cameroon striker and Barcelona teammate between 2004 and 2009

"Messi is a God – as a person and even more so as a player. I hope that he wins the World Cup with Argentina. To the Gods of the world, all I ask is that you give him that chance."

Juan Sebastián Verón
Former Manchester United, Chelsea, and Argentina midfield star

"Every time he grabs the ball and accelerates, I see Maradona. We must protect him. I'd personally put him in a drawer of my bedside table."

David Villa
Former Barça teammate and Spain's all-time leading scorer

"He is doing incredible things. Each day he surprises everyone with a new record, he continually outdoes himself. Nobody can compare with him."

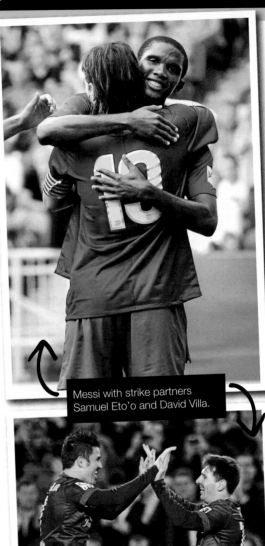

Messi with strike partners Samuel Eto'o and David Villa.

Ossie Ardiles
Former Spurs and Argentina midfield star

"For some time I thought Diego Maradona could never be surpassed, and nor could Pelé, but no longer. I would now say that Lionel Messi will go down in history as the number one player of all time, the best that there ever was."

Ronaldo
Former Barcelona and Brazil striker, and world player of the year in 1996, 1997, and 2002

"He has so much creativity, he enchants us. And despite the fact that he's Argentine, the great rivals of Brazil, he's a player who I admire a great deal. He is the best in the world, so far ahead of the rest. I wish I was 10 years younger so I could play with Messi."

Arsène Wenger
Arsenal manager, against whose team Messi scored all four goals in a 4-1 Champions League victory in 2010

"Messi is like a PlayStation player. He can punish any mistake, make a difference at any moment."

Lionel Messi and Andrés Iniesta celebrate with the trophy following Barcelona's 3-0 defeat of River Plate in the FIFA Club World Cup final in December 2015.

Jupp Heynckes
Former Real Madrid and three-time Bayern Munich coach

"He is a phenomenon. He is in the league of Zinedine Zidane, Diego Maradona, Pelé, and Johan Cruyff. Anyone who scores 50 goals in a season is extraterrestrial."

Carles Puyol
Barcelona teammate 2004–14 and World Cup winner with Spain

"This Barça will be remembered as Messi's Barça. He's well above anything else I've ever seen. He's an alien."

Andrés Iniesta
2010 World Cup winner, Barcelona teammate 2004–18

"His skill, the essence of him as a player, has always been there for all to see. Leo Messi does things that nobody else does."

GREAT GOALS 2

Domestic competition, Champions League, or international soccer — it doesn't matter to Messi, who can score fantastic goals anywhere.

ARGENTINA 4, BRAZIL 3
International friendly, June 9, 2012

Does it get much better than this? Playing against your biggest rivals, five minutes to go, the game locked at 3-3 and if you score one more goal you complete your hat-trick and win the game.

Even a tap-in would have been a fairy-tale ending to the game, but the wizard Messi conjured up something just a little more special.

Messi's first two goals in the game weren't bad, but his third, the match-winner, was simply brilliant. There appeared little danger as he was given the ball out wide near the halfway line, but he immediately skipped past a Brazil defender before racing full speed towards the penalty area.

Then, 25 yards (23 m) out from goal, he unleashed an unstoppable left-footed thunderbolt that flew into the far top corner of the net with Brazil goalkeeper Rafael Barbosa rooted to the spot.

BARCELONA 4, REAL BETIS 2
Primera Division, May 5, 2013

Another perfect example of how Messi can score unforgettable team goals as well as individual goals came in the league match against Real Betis.

Barcelona were leading 3-2 when three of their forward players combined to devastating effect to add a fourth goal and seal the win.

Alexis Sánchez started the move with a pass into Messi near the edge of the penalty box. Messi then played the ball on to Andrés Iniesta, whose fantastic back-heel returned the ball to Alexis, who had run into the area.

Alexis could have shot himself, but he decided to play an perfect pass across goal to Messi, who had got in behind the Betis defense to side-foot home at the far post.

Three players, eight seconds, nine touches, goal. Simply unstoppable.

Messi beats Brazil defender Juan to score his brilliant third goal and clinch a 4-3 win.

Alexis Sánchez and Andrés Iniesta rush to celebrate with Messi after they all played key roles in a great team goal against Real Betis.

BARCELONA 4, AC MILAN 0

Champions League, March 12, 2013

Barcelona looked to be on their way out of the Champions League at the hands of AC Milan after losing the first leg 2-0 in Italy, but Messi had other ideas. He started the fightback with a brilliant goal in the fifth minute of the second leg.

Six different players were involved as Barça moved the ball and looked to drag their opponents out of position. Then, in the blink of an eye, the ball was in the back of the net as Messi played a quick one-two with Xavi on the edge of the box before unleashing a superb curling shot into the top corner of the net. Messi scored again before half-time and Barcelona went on to win 4-0.

Messi celebrates with Dani Alves, Jordi Alba, David Villa, and Andrés Iniesta after scoring against AC Milan.

GREAT MATES

Messi is always the center of attention, but soccer is a team game, and he is part of possibly the greatest team ever to play the game.

While Messi has established himself as the world's top player, he admits he would not have achieved the success he has without the help of his teammates.

He said: "I'm lucky that I get to play here at Barça and for Argentina, where I get to play with fantastic players. They have given me everything: the individual awards, the titles, the goals, everything. Without the help of my teammates, I would be nothing."

A lot of his colleagues at Barcelona (both past and present) have played together for many years, having graduated from the club's famous La Masia academy. Messi explained: "The Barça philosophy isn't about just one coach or another, it's based on an idea, a line that is laid down and all coaches follow. That has always been the way in which the club has worked with the academy."

Such has been the success of Barcelona's youth policy that eight of the players involved in their 2009 Champions League final win over Manchester United had all been at the club as youngsters.

That not only gives all those players a unique sense of commitment and loyalty to the club, it also means Barcelona's famous style of soccer is second nature and makes the team so effective.

Hugely successful

Messi said: "We've been playing together for a long time and we virtually know where the ball's going two or three passes in advance."

The same style of soccer has also been hugely successful for the Spanish national team, which is little surprise when lots of Barcelona players also play for their country.

Messi's pals at the Nou Camp have included Uruguay striker Luis Suárez and Brazil's Neymar. They formed one of the deadliest attacking trios ever seen.

The three stars scored in an incredible 122 goals between them in all competitions during the 2014/15 season as Barça won a famous trophy treble and they were even better in 2015/16 as they shared a jaw-dropping 131 goals.

Messi, Suárez, and Neymar formed an attacking partnership feared by defenses everywhere.

Messi and defender Gerard Piqué have grown up together from the La Masia academy.

"I'm lucky that I get to play here at Barça and for Argentina, where I get to play with fantastic players. They have given me everything."

Messi's childhood hero was Pablo Aimar, who starred for Argentina between 1999 and 2009. Aimar played in the number 10 position and was one of the most skillful players in the world. He started his career at River Plate before time in Spain at Valencia and Real Zaragoza, and then moved to Portugal with Benfica.

June 2004
Following his move to Catalonia and with his super skills in Barcelona's youth teams attracting attention, Messi was offered the chance to play for Spain, but turned it down in order to wait for the call from Argentina. He got it when he was picked in the Under-20 squad for a friendly against Paraguay.

August 17, 2005
Messi's debut for the senior Argentina team lasted less than 60 seconds! The 18-year-old wonderkid had just come on when his shirt was being pulled by Vilmos Vanczák. Messi threw his arm back and the defender went down holding his face. Messi was shown a red card and was soon in tears back in the locker room.

A heartbroken Messi walks off after getting a red card within a minute of coming on for his international debut.

June 16, 2006
Messi stepped off the bench in the group game against Serbia and Montenegro to become the youngest ever Argentina player to appear at the World Cup, aged 18 years and 357 days. He then scored his nation's sixth goal in a 6-0 victory to ensure he is the sixth youngest player to ever score in the tournament.

July 3, 2010
Messi crashes out of his second World Cup still with just one goal to his name in two tournaments. His goal came against Serbia and Montenegro in 2006, but Argentina lost to hosts Germany in the quarter-finals. Four years later it was Germany again who knocked out Messi and his team in South Africa.

August 2011
Messi is named the captain of Argentina at the age of 24 by new manager Alejandro Sabella.

June–July 2014
Messi captains Argentina at the 2014 World Cup in Brazil. He is voted Man of the Match in all three group games as Argentina progress to the final for the first time since 1990, but suffers heartbreak as Mario Götze's 113th-minute strike wins the Cup for Germany.

June 20, 2015
When he wins his 100th cap for Argentina, against Jamaica in the Copa America, Messi becomes only the fifth Argentina player to achieve this amazing milestone.

June 22, 2016
Messi's effort in the 4-0 demolition of hosts United States in the Copa America Centenario takes him to 55 international goals, breaking the Argentina record previously held by Gabriel Batistuta.

Messi became Argentina's all-time top scorer 11 years after making his international debut.

NATIONAL HERO

Messi's career in international soccer with Argentina so far has been a story full of ups and downs — but maybe one day it will have a happy ending.

Compared to the success he has enjoyed with Barcelona, Messi has not managed to do the same with his country – but it could have been very different if he had not stayed loyal to Argentina.

Following his move to Barça and with his potential very clear, Messi was offered the chance to play for Spain, but turned it down in order to wait for his chance with Argentina. He said, "I would have never chosen to play for Spain because I am Argentine."

He got his wish in June 2004 when he was named in Argentina's Under-20 squad for a friendly against Paraguay. His success at the 2005 Under-20 World Cup then saw him get his first call-up to the senior team against Hungary on August 17 at the age of 18.

It was a moment he had been dreaming of for so long, but it soon turned into a nightmare as the wonderkid was brought off the bench in the 63rd minute and shown a red card less than 60 seconds later – a sending-off that left Messi in tears back in the locker room.

He made what he described as a "re-debut" a month later before being handed his first senior start against Peru, and then netting his first goal for his country in a friendly against Croatia in March 2006.

Legend Diego Maradona labelled Messi as his true successor, saying: "I have seen the player who will inherit my place in Argentine football and his name is Messi."

But Messi's memories of his first World Cup in 2006 and Copa America in 2007 would not be happy after two disappointing exits. The lows were soon replaced by the high of 2008 as Messi inspired his country to Olympic gold in Beijing, but further struggles at international level were not far away in the shape of the 2010 World Cup.

Another miserable Copa America followed in 2011, this time on home soil, as Argentina were once more beaten in the quarter-finals.

So close

Messi got both his and Argentina's 2014 World Cup finals campaign off to a flying start, netting the second goal in his side's 2-1 opening-game victory over Bosnia and Herzegovina – his first World Cup finals goal since 2006. He scored a stoppage-time winner in a 1-0 victory over Iran, and twice in a 3-2 victory over Nigeria that saw Argentina top their group. Belief was mounting.

Argentina went on to reach the final for the first time since 1990. But although they enjoyed the better chances against Germany in the final, Mario Götze netted in the 113th minute to bring both Argentina and Messi's dream to a crushing end. The big prize had eluded him once again.

In June 2016, Argentina were beaten in the Copa America final by Chile. After the final, a heartbroken Messi announced he was retiring from international soccer at the age of 29.

The country was in total shock, but after nationwide appeals for him to change his mind, Messi returned to the team in September 2016 and he marked his first game back with the winning goal in a World Cup qualifier against Uruguay.

Messi scored his first senior international goal against Croatia in 2006.

Messi made a brilliant return to international soccer after his short-lived retirement.

"I would have never chosen to play for Spain because I am Argentine."

THE WORLD STAGE

Many people believe Messi cannot truly be regarded as one of the all-time best players in soccer until he has helped his country win the World Cup.

Messi was first selected for World Cup duty in the Argentina squad that traveled to Germany in 2006. After remaining unused for the opening group game, he stepped off the bench in the 75th minute against Serbia and Montenegro. That made him the youngest Argentine ever to appear at the World Cup, aged 18 years and 357 days.

Messi had already set up one goal when he bagged the last in a 6-0 rout to ensure he again wrote his name in the history books as the sixth youngest player ever to score at the tournament.

Yet disappointment was to follow for both Messi and Argentina in the quarter-finals as they crashed out of the competition to hosts Germany on penalties.

Further misery was to come four years later. Argentina had a poor qualification campaign and, with Messi scoring only four times, they only scraped through to the tournament in South Africa. Once there, despite breezing through to the quarter-finals, Argentina were embarrassed 4-0 by Germany once again.

So close to glory

Messi and Argentina would have had high hopes as they traveled to Brazil for the 2014 World Cup. And when the South Americans eased to the top of their group, with Messi picking up the Man of the Match award in every one of three games, expectation started to grow to fever pitch.

Argentina beat Switzerland in the round of 16 (1-0), Belgium in the quarter-finals (1-0), and Holland (5-4 on penalties) in the semi-finals. But the dream came to an end in the final against Germany – a match billed as the world's best player against the world's best team. Germany won the match 1–0, and yet again Messi was left to ponder what might have been.

At the 2018 World Cup in Russia, Argentina finished second in their group to advance to the round of 16. But they lost to France 4–3. Messi did not score in the match but had two assists. France went on to win the tournament.

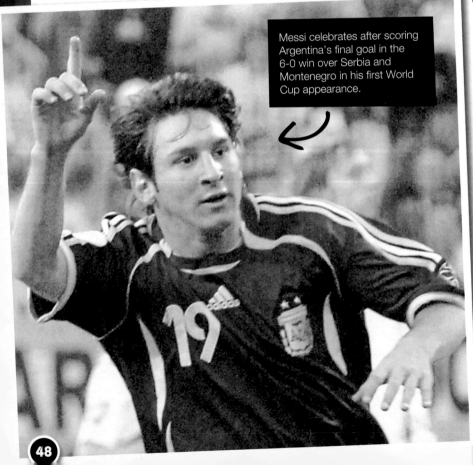

Messi celebrates after scoring Argentina's final goal in the 6-0 win over Serbia and Montenegro in his first World Cup appearance.

Messi scored his first World Cup finals goal against Serbia and Montenegro in Germany in the 2006 finals.

10 AND OUT

Messi scored against Venezuela in qualifying for the 2010 World Cup after being given the famous number 10 shirt for the first time by new coach Diego Maradona, but Argentina's trip to the finals in South Africa brought more misery. They got through to the quarter-finals again, but once more Germany stood in their way and this time they powered to a 4-0 win to leave Messi and Argentina distraught.

Messi celebrates scoring against Venezuela in qualifying – his first game in the number 10 shirt for Argentina.

Argentina's 2010 FIFA World Cup 4-0 quarter-final defeat against Germany left Messi bitterly disappointed – and in need of a hug from coach Diego Maradona.

Messi found his goal scoring touch at the 2014 World Cup, but Argentina's World Cup dreams lay in tatters after they lost in the final to Germany.

COACH PARTY

Messi has played under several coaches and managers during his club and international career and has not failed to impress any of them.

Pep Guardiola

Led Barcelona to an amazing period of success with 14 trophies in just four seasons and played a key role in helping Messi develop into the best player in the world.

"Like Michael Jordan in basketball, Messi is dominating his sport. Very few people in history have managed to dominate their sport the way Jordan and Messi have.

"I feel sorry for those who want to compete for Messi's throne – it's impossible, this kid is unique. He doesn't just score lots of goals, but he scores lots of great goals, each one being better than the last.

"The throne belongs to him, and no one else but him will decide when he vacates it. He's the best there is. There's no one else. I can count myself lucky to have been his coach."

Former Holland international star Frank Rijkaard was the Barcelona coach who gave Messi his first-team chance.

Frank Rijkaard

Gave Messi his Barcelona debut during his time in charge at the Nou Camp between 2003 and 2008.

"He's an incredible person. Messi is not simply a uniquely talented footballer. He's also strong mentally, very bright and exceptionally dedicated to his job.

"Personally speaking I enjoy watching him play and I'm deeply proud of him and what he has achieved. Quite simply, he's the best."

Messi made his Barcelona debut the season after Luis Enrique ended his Nou Camp playing career.

Edgardo Bauza
Former Argentina manager.
"What surprised me is how much he knows about football, because he knows everything, about his teammates, the technical team, about football. He's aware of everything. Nothing escapes him."

"I think it would be a sin not to give Messi to the people, to the team"

– Diego Maradona, Argentina coach 2008–2010

Luis Enrique
Barcelona manager between 2014 and 2017 who won seven major trophies during his eight years as a player at the Nou Camp.
"Messi is the best in the world without any doubt and for me the history of football. He does not really seem human to me."

GLOBAL SUPERSTAR

Messi is now undeniably the best player in the modern game, and it has made him recognizable all over the world.

His obvious qualities on the field as well as his humble and gracious attitude have made Lionel Messi a role model for millions of fans. The Argentine has twice been included in *Time* magazine's famous annual list of the 100 most influential people in the world. Messi has sponsorship deals with big companies like adidas, Pespi, and EA Sports (the makers of the FIFA computer game), all of which have all boosted his earning power. In 2018, *Forbes* magazine listed him as the second highest paid athlete on the planet.

In April 2011, Messi launched a Facebook page that by 2019 had attracted 89 million likes. He also has a Twitter page and an Instagram account, and according to a 2016 survey, Messi's social media audience was more than 122 million across all three platforms.

Famous waxwork museum Madame Tussauds made a life-size figure of the Barcelona forward for both its London and New York locations.

Goodwill ambassador

Nicknamed "the flea" due to his size, speed and balance, Messi has also been the subject of more wacky adulation including the pure gold replica of his magical left foot on sale in Japan.

Charity work forms a large part of Messi's life, especially helping out kids in need. It includes the Leo Messi Foundation he set up in 2007 to help

A fan poses with the wax figure of Messi at the Madame Tussauds exhibition in Tokyo.

Messi also spends much of his free time doing charity work. In 2010 he was named as a goodwill ambassador for UNICEF.

vulnerable children and his role as a goodwill ambassador for the United Nations Children's Fund (UNICEF).

Despite the fact that he is not as well known in the United States, where American football, baseball, basketball, and ice hockey are more popular, Messi still made the headlines in 2011 when President Barack Obama mentioned him in a speech. Then, in 2016, he sent signed shirts to the president's daughters Malia and Sasha after they revealed they were big fans.

GREAT GOALS 3

And the great goals kept on coming from Messi — at the World Cup, in La Liga, and in the Champions League. No stage, it seems, is too grand for the Argentine maestro.

BARCELONA 5, SEVILLA 1

Premiera Division, November 22, 2014

This was not so much the goal itself, but the significance of it. Throughout the early part of the 2014/15 season, Messi had been hunting down Telmo Zarra's all-time goal scoring record in La Liga – 251 goals in a 15-year career for Athletic Bilboa between 1940 and 1955. And as the Argentine drew closer, the clamor became louder. By the time Barcelona faced Sevilla in La Liga at the Nou Camp on November 22, Messi was just one goal behind. He opened the scoring with a trademark free-kick in the first half to equal the record, and then, in the 71st minute, with Barcelona leading 3-1, he tapped in from short range following a Barça breakaway to set a new mark. His teammates responded by gathering around Messi, picking him up and hurling him into the air.

BARCELONA 3, BAYERN MUNICH 0

Champions League, May 6, 2015

Bayern Munich had provided stubborn resistance to Barcelona in the first leg of the Champions League semi-final at the Nou Camp. As the match entered the final quarter, the scores were locked at 0-0. And then Messi worked his magic. He opened the scoring in the 77th minute, but it was his second goal three minutes later that got people talking. He picked up the ball on the left-hand edge of the penalty area, feigned to go left but went right, leaving Bayern Munich defender Jérôme Boateng on the floor, and then produced a chip of outlandish quality over the advancing Manuel Neuer (the best goalkeeper in the world) to score.

Messi's second goal against Sevilla saw him break Telmo Zarra's all-time La Liga goal scoring record.

Messi's goal against Sporting Gijón underlined his status as La Liga's deadliest marksman of all time.

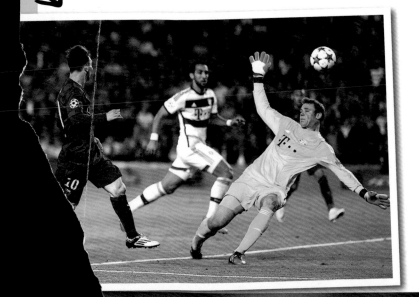

A touch of class: Manuel Neuer is left grasping thin air as Messi produces a sublime chip against Bayern Munich.

SPORTING GIJÓN 1, BARCELONA 3

La Liga, February 17, 2016

Messi has always done things in style throughout his record-breaking career and it was no different when he became the first-ever player to score 300 goals in La Liga. His historic strike came in the 24th minute of the match against Sporting Gijón. He collected the ball 40 yards from goal and beat two defenders with a drop of the shoulder and a trademark burst of pace. Messi was still outside the area, but a glorious left-footed drive, which rocketed into the bottom corner, was a typically brilliant effort to take him to the landmark of 300 La Liga goals.

March 7, 2012
Becomes the first player to score five goals in a Champions League game as Barcelona thrashes Bayer Leverkusen 7-1.

May 12, 2012
Finishes the season with an incredible 50 goals in the league – a Primera División record and also beating the previous best mark to win the European Golden Shoe, which was the 47 goals scored by Romanian Dudu Georgescu for Dinamo Bucharest in 1976/77.

Dec. 9, 2012
Breaks the record for the most goals in a calendar year with his double against Real Betis taking him to 86 in all competitions for Barcelona and Argentina, overtaking Bayern Munich and Germany legend Gerd Müller's record from 1972. Messi ended 2012 with a breathtaking 91 goals.

Jan. 7, 2013
Becomes the first soccer player to win FIFA's World Player of the Year/Ballon d'Or award four times after being named the best player on the planet for the fourth successive year.

RECORD BREAKER

March 30, 2013
Messi becomes the first player in Primera División history to score in consecutive matches against every other team in the division after netting for the 19th successive league game in the 2-2 draw with Celta Vigo.

November 22, 2014
Scores 252nd La Liga goal to become the highest scorer in the competition's history.

Sept. 16, 2015
Makes his 100th appearance in the UEFA Champions League for Barça against Roma. At 28 years and 84 days old, he's the youngest player to reach the 100-game mark in UCL history.

Nov. 30, 2015
Messi is voted La Liga's best player for 2015. It's a record sixth time he has won the award after first picking up the trophy in 2009.

Jan. 11, 2016
Is announced as the 2015 FIFA Ballon d'Or winner, the first man to receive the famous award five times.

WHAT NEXT?

What does the future hold for Messi? What is there still to achieve for a man who won more individual and club medals and awards before his 30th birthday than most players achieve in their whole careers?

Although he holds records such as the all-time scoring record in La Liga, Lionel Messi still has plenty to play for in the rest of his career. How many more goals can he score? How many more winner's medals can he collect?

There is also his ambition to win the World Cup, to emulate what many of his Barcelona teammates have done with Spain and what his hero Diego Maradona did with Argentina in 1986.

As for where he might play in the future, Messi has never shown any desire to leave Barcelona for another top European club. He said in 2012: "This is my home, my club. I owe everything to Barça. I'm very happy here."

However, he has also spoken about potentially returning to play in Argentina. "I would love to return," he said, in 2016 when asked if he would ever re-sign for his first club, Newell's Old Boys. "It is something I have kept an eye on because it was my dream as a child. Obviously my life started to change and went another way but I have no regrets. It's something I have kept an eye on. I want to play in Argentine football and Newell's, where I grew up."

Once he does stop playing, Messi will be able to reflect properly on all the amazing things that have happened to him during his time in the game.

As he says: "I don't think it will be until after I've retired that I'm fully aware of what I've done or what I've achieved in my career."

There is one thing Messi is hoping to guarantee before he hangs up his jersey, though – that he is remembered by future generations for all the right reasons.

Spectacular goals

"I'm more concerned about being a good person than being the best footballer in the world," he said. "My hope is that when I retire that I'm remembered as a good guy."

But even if Messi does finish without breaking any more records or scoring any more spectacular goals, he has still already done more than enough to entertain millions of soccer fans, and then we can all bid him farewell and simply say: "Lionel Andrés Messi, thanks for the memories."

Spectacular goals have given Messi's fans plenty of memories to treasure.

"This is my home, my club. I owe everything to Barça. I'm very happy here."

KNOW YOUR STUFF

Here are 20 questions to test your Messi knowledge. All of the answers can be found somewhere in the book!

1 What is Messi's middle name?

2 In which Argentine city was Messi born?

3 Against which team did Messi score five goals in a single Champions League match in 2012?

4 Which of the following players has played alongside Messi for Argentina: Zlatan Ibrahimović, Ángel Di María or David Villa?

5 At what age did Messi score his first competitive goal for Barcelona in 2005?

6 Who were the same opponents in the final when Barcelona won the 2009 and 2011 Champions League titles?

7 Name Messi's first two first-team managers at Barcelona.

8 What date is Messi's birthday?

9 Messi beat the record of which former Germany striker when he scored 91 goals in 2012?

10 How many league goals did Messi score during the 2011/12 season?

11 Against which La Liga club did the teenaged Messi make his Barça debut in 2004?

12 Against which team did Messi score his record-breaking 300th La Liga goal?

13 How many times has the Argentina superstar won the FIFA Ballon d'Or?

14 Messi made his 100th appearance in the Champions League against which Italian team?

15 How old was Messi when he was given his first soccer ball?

16 In what year did Messi score the winning goal against Estudiantes in Abu Dhabi to earn Barcelona their first-ever FIFA Club World Cup crown?

17 The striker was in brilliant form in 2015 as Barcelona lifted the Champions League trophy to complete a famous treble. Which side did they beat in the final?

18 Name the two players who combined with Messi to score 131 goals in the 2015/16 season.

19 How old was Messi when he became Argentina's youngest-ever player in the World Cup when he came off the bench against Serbia and Montenegro in 2006?

20 In what year did Messi win an Olympic gold medal with Argentina?

Quiz answers

1 Andrés; 2 Rosario; 3 Bayer Leverkusen; 4 Ángel Di María; 5 17 years old; 6 Manchester United; 7 Frank Rijkaard and Pep Guardiola; 8 June 24; 9 Gerd Müller; 10 50; 11 Espanyol; 12 Sporting Gijón; 13 Five; 14 AS Roma; 15 Four; 16 2009; 17 Juventus; 18 Luis Suárez & Neymar; 19 18; 20 2008.

accolade An award of acknowledgment or praise.

adulation Extreme or excessive admiration or praise.

archrival A person or team's main rival, or person or team they are trying to beat.

clamor A loud noise.

emulate To try to be like someone, usually because you admire them.

equalizer A score that ties a game.

feign To pretend or fake.

friendly A game between teams that is not part of the regular season and is not part of the normal league or championship play.

maestro A person who is a master or an expert in a field, often in an art.

slalom To move in a zigzag.

successive When something happens one after another; in a row.

treble When a team wins three trophies in a season.

triumph A great victory; also to achieve such a victory.

vacate To leave.

FOR FURTHER READING

Books

Burshtein, Karen. *Lionel Messi: Soccer's Top Scorer*. New York, NY: Britannica Educational Publishing, 2016.

Cooperson, Jeremy, and Brian Wingate. *An Insider's Guide to Soccer*. New York, NY: Rosen Central, 2015.

Jökulsson, Illugi. *Stars of World Soccer*. New York, NY: Abbeville Press Publishers, 2018.

McCollum, Sean. *Full STEAM Soccer: Science, Technology, Engineering, Arts, and Mathematics of the Game*. North Mankato, MN: Capstone Press, 2019.

Websites

FC Barcelona
www.fcbarcelona.com/en/football/first-team/players/4974/lionel-messi
Read more about Messi on the FC Barcelona website.

FIFA
www.fifa.com
Find all the most up-to-date news about soccer around the world on FIFA's website.

Sports Illustrated Kids
www.sikids.com/soccer
Keep up with the latest happenings in soccer on the Sports Illustrated Kids website.

INDEX